Expert Writing &

Teaching Authors, Writers, Business People with Totally New Insights

Think about this - - - The **written word** and its companion, the PRINTED PAGE, go back almost **500 years** - to the time of Johannes Gutenberg and his all-to amazing hand-operated printing press ~ The year was 1540, over 100 years before the Mayflower flotilla crossed the Atlantic Ocean and tacked into the future Boston Bay Harbor.

We modern day folks have come to take printed words for granted to the extent, if you will, fast forward to 2017 with me to see some very smart people have transformed the written word into electronic bits and bytes allowing us to read the word on our computers, tablets, phones and wrist watches; and now on the interior of glass automobile windshields – **Beyond unique!** And you say 'I want to be a part of this'– *Yes, you do!!!*

Let's explore and give you a chance - call me!

Scott Brown

661-394-0000
Nova Publishing & Book Store
Bakersfield, California

Dedicated to all

enthused, inspired writers -

Ready to advance your cause

throughout this entire

amazing Planet

Expect Gratifying Results,

Learn to control your own

writing destiny

Preface

Greetings fellow authors, published or not, completed book or not; yet willing and ready!!!

I have stood where you stand today in this lovely, yet lonely field of writing prose, fiction, history, or company news. I know your keen desires . . . And you must sustain these desires to move forward to your chosen legacy.

> **Here is 'the good news'** – Today recognize you can achieve your very own dream book in a matter of days, weeks or months and arrive at this station in life as I have – Being a writer for others to read your works for study, enjoyment, fulfillment or daily news. You can and will reach your literary goals.

Your book will come together when you are committed, enthusiastic, and show the integrity due to yourself and due to others to write, write, write . . . for their benefit and yours.

I know you are eager, excited and full of wonder, and at times – doubt. Will I make it? All the way to publication? Do I have what it takes?

This book is all about that 'what it takes.'

Read on and absorb for your ride to success.

Expert Writing & Publishing -
Teaching Authors, Writers, Business People with Totally New Insights

Table of Contents

Table of Contents
Continued

Chapter 1

My Perspective – Your way to success

Can you remember **the excitement and wonder you felt when you were first struck with the notion of 'writing'?** Perhaps something bigger than a magazine article? Perhaps a long treasured piece like a book?

I do, really, quite well. I was about forty-five years younger, in my early thirties. How old were you? Reflect on your answer with me because we will see how all of these thoughts come into play for your success. And age is totally immaterial.

For me it was 1973. **I was up in the mountains of Nevada**, a 'ghost town hotel night manager' - truth. I had pared down my possessions. Up there my first writing desk was a chest of drawers as you may have in your bedroom, where I had turned the top drawer upside down, slid it back in partway and placed my trusty Royal portable typewriter on it. That make-shift tabletop thrilled me, I was ready.

For my first book I knew I had a great subject, great storyline and great determination. What I didn't know was I 'won't be committed' - for the long haul - to complete a book. As a matter of fact, I ran out of steam very quickly; within weeks. Sound like anything you have confronted?

Why would I have you read this important book of encouragement by first presenting you with a factual story of struggle? Let's keep moving and find the answer.

A lot of maturing and travels have passed since my early adventures of authoring. These days, **I love to write. The Words fly out of my fingertips. I'm definitely committed.** Sound more like you?

I wake up at all times of the night, or shift my priorities during the day, to sit down and write. I love sending a page to the printer and proofreading my own thoughts. I love experiencing what the reader will imagine, or see, or close his or her eyes to just muse and wonder about my characters.

Where are you in this mix of joy, talent, knowledge and fluttering in your stomach when you cruise back into your vivid mind and start thinking again about writing? If you 'zoned out' just 5 minutes ago when you took your hands off the keyboard for a break - - - are you now focused again?

Are you still excited? Still eager?

If so, here is 'How we are going to make a big difference in your writing and publishing':

I am going to introduce you to our Nova

- Success Planning Studies –

Nova's Success Plan refers to a simple toolset of your own personal faculties and traits which I call enacting '**Success Planning**' on your very own!

Let me tell you right off the bat, in our time together which you are allowing me, I will educate you on how really 'simple and inexpensive' book publishing can be with us!!!

So, here at this beginning step, lets search for your own personal answers to **Success Planning with your –**

First Significant Writing 'Key Fact'

As an important lead-off to your writing career, I am going to explain to you the simple tools you already have and how you can proceed with sharpening your opportunity for success even before we venture into the 'what and how' you will learn to become a great, long-term writer.

Are you with me? Are you ready for Success???

If I may let me explain to you about a most extraordinary time in my life when I experienced a huge change. I was 55 years young, out of high school for 37 years, graduated from college 32 years earlier - Do the math - even after 5 years of college it took 32 years for this BIG change.

Here's how - I had been working alongside a really sharp oil company project manager for 4 plus years. Evert was showing me how to make smart, timely decisions as we figured out daily how his new multi-million dollar plant would operate. I took notes and talked 'modern plant control systems' constantly with him.

After that assignment ended, my mind was milling over our successes of that huge project and one morning I jumped out of bed saying to myself, "I got it!" - I knew that our own personal actions, or **traits** were the basis of what moved us forward to success.

What was this all about? What had I stumbled on - Some kind of perfection – some kind of doing it and doing it right? – Each and every time?

What was this thinking 'that was coming through' to me? Within a matter of 3 or 4 days, I mapped out a collection of **Six human traits that** each and **every one of us embodies in our minds**.

Evert had shown me - it was '**Commitment'**. And then as I connected the dots, one idea of knowing led to another idea of knowing, and soon the good news fell together perfectly – more than I first realized!!!

Why? Because as it turned out - **Success Planning** for any task, and especially writers, will always include **Six Milestones** [as shown in boxes on Page 6] that fully define capabilities already residing in each of us - **'to be all we can be'** –

Equally importantly, these traits couple-up together for **the synergy to stay on track, and in our case, to effectively and completely create our dream book**. I call them Milestone Traits **as they 'always lay ahead** of us **to be achieved'** . . . And we most likely have not been engaging or even aware of all six working together so well for us.

This was my fresh look at 'commitment'. Actual real **Commitment - get the job done exactly as the client wanted it done**. Evert had given me great responsibilities to assist and participate.

He had taught me to **Commit – Partake – Get it done**.

Next please see **Page 6** for the full listings of the

Success Planning Studies

Here are the **Six Milestone Traits** you need to **assure becoming a full-fledged author**.

Writer's Milestone 1 - Commitment

Commitment
- You are totally engaged as if your life and very being count on it. In fact, they do count, really.
- Your Success is all about being committed to your cause - moving toward results
---

-You are Committed to completing your writing, printing, and publishing assignments, <u>your book</u>

Milestone 2 - Enthusiasm

Enthusiasm
-You feel and show enthusiasm at all times
-This particular trait is rare and very important for you and a big following of your best clients
---

-Others see it, feel it, and join in your enthusiasm wanting to be part of it. Be enthused, enjoy too!

Milestone 3 - Integrity

Integrity
-You must understand the requirement of moral thinking, do it without exception.
-You welcome integrity, You are known for it. Think of Integrity as going the extra mile!

-You illustrate this in every action especially when temptation pulls you differently

Milestone 4 - Natural Talent

> ### * Natural Talent
> -You have one special talent that is a gift to you at birth - it is there to find, use, and include.
> -Using this one singular talent will serve you best every time. Mine – **Visionary** (& *organization-I got 2*)

-Satisfaction can be felt as you find, use, and release that special talent – Will yours serve writing?

Milestone 5 - Persistence

> ### Persistence
> -Success demands the job is done completely, 100% (Enjoy - don't trudge with perseverance)
> -The job and its tasks must go to completion –
> Be persistent. Use your talent, **REACH 100%**

-You must have the will and determination to do it, bringing you forward with staying power

Milestone 6 - Reward

> ### Reward
> -The dangling carrot is part of your reason for service, it's your Reward - It will come when you serve and reward others with your writing - - -
> -Your whole being must coexist in commitment and reward – never forget this!!! Own It.

-Yes, please remember you deserve the reward **you will and can earn!** Go long (Baseball term for **Homerun**)

Put these **Six Traits** to work for you!!!

Chapter 2

Creative Insights – Enjoying writing!

We move ahead in this chapter <u>to put **your very own success traits and talent to work**</u> – <u>It is time to introduce the variables that will make and grow you as a good writer with a perfect book.</u>

<u>I will continually encourage you to refer to our six traits to assure yourselves of milestone progress, so that you are achieving maximum benefit of your time learning or re-learning to write and then publish.</u>

From this point on I will number and title subjects for your referral when questions arise.

Key Point 1 – <u>Why I write?</u>

Let's talk about why you can and will become a great writer. I am sure you are curious to hear my words and compare them to yours.

<u>I am going to ask you each why you choose to write. What can you tell me? Here are some ideas.</u>

My readers can see themselves in the story, as I do enjoying life through 'my characters', their dialogues, ups/downs, with emotional, moving, happy endings.

I re-live, re-learn special points each day as I write what I can intertwine with profound meaning for my readers.

I experience great 'ah-ha's as I write, ones I may need, and strive to colorfully write them for my readers.

Can you see the ribbon <u>woven in by my ideas</u> – Readers are vital, and I enjoy writing for them.

Key Point 2 – <u>I am always focused on my readers' pleasure and satisfaction</u>

In my work going forward with a new book **'Readers are integral', <u>they are our life-blood and push us forward.</u>** He/she is my audience. Give them hours of pleasurable reading to feel redeemed when they close the back cover.

<u>Suggestion</u> – **<u>Always think of the reader</u>, giving him/her easy, non-repetitive reading, with lively, colorful characters, back and forth conversations and dialogue that leaves readers asking for more, wanting the characters back. Dodge long paragraphs like the plague.

Key Point 3 – <u>Your life's adventures will feed your writing</u>.

<u>Use them for the wide variety they represent. Write your feelings. Entwine your characters in these events as 'strong moments'.</u>

We will soon list all the steps and methods, as well as page by page building of your book. So at this early stage of coaching you, please realize that writing is also for your moment by moment pleasure - This talent, this gift is yours to enjoy.

Make the most of your commitment to learn to get great satisfaction from each word you search and lay down, from each page completed, and chapter printed for review. Time will reward you, let words flow from your fingertips, as they do mine. Edits will follow to assist with easy reading.

These words of mine here in chapter 2 are extraordinarily important for you to own to bring you comfort and understanding as you become and remain a very successful author by constantly writing for your reader from your heart.

If (a word I don't use often, nor do I even like), If you want to become and stay a writer authoring books, the main component you must achieve is a good yarn (old fashion word) of a story that captures attention and keeps the readers hunkered around the campfire listening, reading, a good story. Please keep this in mind – Remind yourself.

So, now as we explore the steps we must take to fulfill this role as an author, please think of yourself as someone with a well-crafted, intriguing story that folks have spent time to find and now are totally in your hands to keep.

I trust you see a theme - Three Key Elements - Use your life and its gifts for the wide variety they represent, coalesce real and imagined events from your travels, from your everyday fun and excitement of life, and from your vivid imagination. Write your feelings and be kind – don't rake yourself and your readers over the coals. It is your time to concentrate on success at what makes a good writer and a perfect book.

Chapter 3

Basic Knowhow – Path to the book market

Good Morning – let's open Day 2 by reviewing our **First Significant Writing Key Fact** – We found it is all about **your natural talent and 6 success planning traits that you already possess. And more importantly, it's about how you will develop those traits as you stretch to be a writer.**

Key Point 4 – Use our **Success Planning Studies to 'control and own your part in your personal success'**. I hardily advise you keep these words close by – **Commitment, Enthusiasm, Integrity, Natural Talent, Persistence, Reward**

Remember - each one of these is a human trait within you - used together they constantly hone your capacity to do all tasks you elect successfully; so here we go, this is what we are doing next - digging into our lesson of 'Writing and Publishing is easy and inexpensive'.

I know you most certainly want to ask the question, 'How is easy and inexpensive possible?' Here's a brief listing of my 'History of Book Writing and Publishing' to illustrate what I mean.

This recap gives us the true view of what it took for me to place 5 of my books up on Amazon, and then another 5 by new authors, soon to be 10 books. These authors came to Nova Publishing for help to stop the ordeal of long tedious writing, editing and **anxiety of the old way of sending off manuscripts fearing 'Rejection Slips' in return**.

Key Point 5 – <u>Your Author's First Main-Step – Love of Writing</u>

➢ I look upon sitting and writing for hours as a gift. I can express with pleasure and fulfillment weaving words into sentences, sentences into paragraphs, and paragraphs into chapters, all adding up to tell the story. I love to see words ebb onto the screen!

➢ I personally take this to heart, thinking of my writing as a mission I have been assigned to bring joy, enlightenment, the possibility of redemption, even recovery from levels of dis-satisfaction in my readers' lives.

➢ In turn, this is a now a new skill that I may otherwise not have known, comes alive. Early on I was presented with the joy two of my lady readers felt from my first book, *Nine Lives, Nine Loves*. After diligently reading and marking each chapter, they eagerly returned for the next, voicing their love of my stories – Do you know what that did for me ~ I wanted to write and write more.

I am blessed as my **integrity, commitment, and enthusiasm** each assure the completion of stories! '<u>Words readily flow out my fingertips.</u>' When I am at the keyboard, I do not suffer writer's block!!! These Key Points are the inner powers of writing for you to use and grow your natural talent!! **Next:**

Second Significant Writing 'Key Fact'

Key Point 6 – <u>Your Author's Second Main-Step</u> is learning today's DIGITAL TECHNOLOGY! This is equally important for your '**ease of being a great published author'** and we will teach you!

Simply stated, Nova Publishing utilizes **Digital Technology as the means by which we convert your PC generated Word document, aka your manuscript, <u>into a finished appearing book</u>** and do so '**<u>right before your eyes on your very own PC screen!'</u>** And this is . . .

- Done even before hitting the printing press! -

➢ **<u>Did you have any idea</u>, <u>or know any of these</u> Wonderful actions are possible?** No? – Okay, then I'll bet you can't wait to see your words become a real book!!!

➢ **<u>How can this mystery of the publishing world happen?</u> Answer**: '<u>With a Computer Template that actually mimics the layout of a printed book</u>' which we help you setup.

➢ Then next, **<u>YOUR TEMPLATE DRIVES a $60,000 PRINTING PRESS</u>** (Well it's not a press these days) <u>It's an amazing mega-high</u>

speed copier/printer like yours at home, yet **Bigger and Smarter which 'in few steps' creates a fine book from your Word file!**

➢ And this 'final book printing action' takes place each time an order is entered on an internet site like our Nova Publishing.org.

➢ **The moment after your fully developed book template file is uploaded to reside on our favorite print firm's computer server,** *an order placed on our internet Nova Book Store triggers our website computer to send emails to* **1.)** our assigned printing company to produce your book, **2.)** to the buyer as verification, **3.)** to our order entry group declaring the book title, quantity purchased, sales price, shipping method, ship-to-address, likely date of arrival, **and 4.)** to one other 'Nova staff member' to assure everyone in the loop is happy!!!

➢ **Are you beginning to feel the 'easy factor'** I have been talking about? What's more is our company assists you in loading your manuscript into the template and we align, space, punctuate, spell and grammar check for you. Your book template is almost done.

➢ During setup of your book you will pick its physical size, title, fonts and special highlighting. You, with our team, will load your Word 'electronic manuscript', save it, stored your resultant Portable Digital File (PDF) as a look-alike book on your PC and our server - **with unbelievable excitement**!

➢ You will **proof your manuscript** in the book template and see the actual book appearance from page to page, and cover to cover.

Key Point 7 – <u>Other Current Technology thoughts</u> to bring us out from behind the Wizard's Curtain in the Emerald City of Oz - - -

➢ Nova has welcomed a book printing partner whose staff members are the everyday working people actually converting your computer file to a beautifully printed, perfectly crafted glossy cover book. They print, cut to the perfect size, package, label and ship your book direct to your buyer.

➢ We set this relationship up from the knowledge gained in my writing career when I said, "<u>I am going to contract my own book manufacturer</u>" to satisfy a nagging feeling 'From here forward I'm choosing not to pay for any assistance in accomplishing my dream. That was 10 plus years ago. The results have been seamless.

➢ Through a lot of research and phone calls I narrowed this important selection of a book printer down to an industry favorite. The next step was to set up our own account to register my books and Nova authors' books, load them on their server, and buy them at the printing company's agreed wholesale sell price. Our books are then 'printed on demand' for one, twenty, or 100 online sales for any of us at Nova; making future sales at book shows or special events again easy.

➢ So, we have come to a place in your writing career in conceiving your first book where we will sign you up with our excellent printing house for all these same reasons, making you ready to receive online royalty payments and keep close watch on your own book sales accounting.

As your book takes on a life of its own with 'these tech steps we will walk the technology path' and stand together at your Author's Great Place 1, with your book files ready to go to the printers!

This said, the best news - Nova asks just a $50 Service Charge per book for all these steps, and there is NO set up cost for the printing. You, at last, sense the easy, low cost factor? Good - -

Now with these setup activities explained, the **Next Set of Learning Skills puts you 'front and center'** at the keyboard of your PC to commence practicing writing composition activities!!!

Chapter 4

Take time for Learning the exact steps

Now for another really significant step, Nova is pleased to offer you **an effortless way to write your book**. We will move forward with added Key Points of four ESSENTIAL LESSONS WITH DETAILED STEPS. Are you ready for more surprises and tips?

Key Point 8 – Writing a book is comprised of learning and using sequential steps.

In these essential Nova Lessons I have gathered together **sequential steps** that you can follow to mature your in-depth knowledge of the 'art of writing' – These are Steps I assembled and have used over many years. At the end of these steps we will have revealed and set in action simple here-to-fore muted secrets about writing. I know you will always find and uncover more questions that will keep you learning and asking for more, so please call us when those questions arise.

Lesson 1 – Believing in the Ease of Writing

Welcome now as we dig into the 'What and How' you need in your repertoire to personally become a proficient writer 'with ease'. These lessons and steps will help you learn a method that **eliminates trial and error and brings you satisfying results**.

<u>**Learning Step 1**</u> - Right up front let me assure you the greatest advantage and best news is based on a safe assumption **you already own a PC or Apple computer with Microsoft Word as your Word Processor Software.** True? – With a Yes, <u>You are already Half-way There to building your book</u>!

The reason I can say 'half-way there' is that you <u>will compose your manuscript **on your PC just** exactly like the **'finished book pages' will look!**</u>

<u>**This is our 'secret agent' exposed – You will use a visual book 'pathway and presentation' that sets you at ease the entire time you write**</u>. You are always look at your book layout – Big advantage.

<u>Therefore, as a serious author</u>, please own your own PC <u>and do not share it with others. You must be free to use your PC at any time</u>. **You will be thrilled with the 'ease the PC provides to step-up your composing and editing' – So improved over struggling to build your manuscript with** pencil and paper; and changes and updates are a breeze.

<u>**Step 2**</u> – Even better news, **as a Credible Author you no longer <u>need to labor over an 8½ x 11 inch double spaced 'rough draft' submission</u>** (With Nova's process no one critiques your work). <u>Print books are easy to produce because **your PC Microsoft Word .doc file** is also our printing company's go-to-file, using it just as you saved and uploaded it. They will review it to assure we</u>

have set it up per their printing format approval.

As we progress together here with these sequential steps, know that your Word .doc file can be emailed to others whom you pick, and trust to read and check your early composition for readability.

Training Point - **Your ability to craft a 'readable story' is 'essential'** for fans to enjoy easy reading just as you enjoy easy authoring. **We will cover more on these two very Key Lesson Steps shortly.**

Step 3 – Let's talk straight talk on being a successful writer, specifically a well-loved writer! Remember this - Being a prolific writer is a talent you may be born with and will always sharpen!

Wanting to be a good writer is half of the challenge - Training yourself to be a great one is the other half!!! Here is my list of **Power of 7** ways to remind yourself of this constant striving to be an EXCELLENT WRITER – you can copy it, keep it close at hand, rely on it, and be committed to it:

1. **It is best to love story crafting** – truly enjoy each word, sentence, page – This is your expanded writer's gift to yourself.

2. **Begin by picking a genre' you like!** For your early benefit **list the characters & Table of Contents** – Use these, to 'feel if you have a fit-up' coming together with your chosen genre'.

3. <u>Remember</u> 'the always available PC' and '<u>a quiet place to write</u>'. You owe yourself a writer's space for your creative soul to blossom and grow. Schedule times without a cell phone or visitors.

4. <u>Dedication,</u> be prepared for devoting hours to story building - you write, you edit and delete, and you do it over - - - again don't worry, it will come.

5. <u>Always learn</u>, look for classes from great authors. I just took one, got lots of red marks on my essay that will help me. More is always good on the learning curve.

6. <u>Write for the reader</u>. <u>Your 'book is not one without readers'</u>. **Stop** long sentences, paragraphs, reader boredom, and your reader skipping ahead.

7. And **<u>Here is Lucky Number 7</u> - that you will never forget – '<u>Edit your book 7 times</u>'!**

I know it sounds tough – with my *'**Writer's Power of Seven**'* all authors do multiple edits for each of their books. **Believe me, your book gets better and better with each edit, and you feel good and rewarded. Edit often for readability**. Believe me!!!

For those who want a **Homework assignment –Copy this <u>Power of Seven List</u> above, or make your own.**

<u>**Carry it with you.**</u>

<u>Study it for 21 days.</u>

<u>During this time please do as I suggest</u> - <u>list your characters, create that important initial Table of Contents. You will see why</u> – <u>all these items are vital, they will grow and morph</u>! Watch and see!

<u>Lesson 2</u> - "Going Deeper into the Layers of Writing and Publishing"

<u>Important</u> - Trust there will be wonderful moments of elating Ah-ha's as your output improves. <u>On your quest to becoming a published author you will find digging deeper is really about</u> **"perfecting relatively few steps and methods"**.

Think repetition of writing and re-writing on your part to improve each story, each character, and to rapidly expand your ability to imagine it, write it, and write it again with more intrigue.

When you go back to edit **think to yourself 'there are at least three ways to write the same material, paragraph, and make the point more climactic'**.

Going Deeper Alert - <u>Now that you have had time to assess the rigors of being a successful author let me tell you what other people see about expert writing in this 21st Century</u> - **They ask, "Are you ON the Cutting Edge of Publication?"** **Here at Nova - The answer is YES**, and we want that for you. That is why you are here to learn – From this point forward **what we are going to teach you in Lesson 2 will stick 'if you believe you are Half Way here'!** So, do you believe? <u>**Do you have your own Computer up and running now**</u>? Just checking.

If so, **I can assure you of <u>Two Events that will absolutely stun you</u>,** <u>'Putting you beyond belief into the big league' and set you up for a huge win.</u>

Event #1 – <u>You will cheer, cry, smile, call a friend, write your mother, all to tell them, **"I will be published! Yes? YES!**</u> This moment is within reach and is so good, like your first bike ride, graduation from high school, leaning over the rim of the Grand Canyon, holding your breath while immersed in its grandeur and endless beauty, so go ahead and say it. Test how it feels, **"I will be published!"**

Event #2 – <u>And then</u>, just like the always bigger, better, famous LA Auto Show with the unveiling of the very latest 'Year 2020 driverless, Solar Electric Minicar **causing 'thousands of people to gasp', the same will happen for you when <u>'you see your dream book in living color on a sales web page'</u> for the <u>VERY FIRST TIME</u>. <u>Trust me, you will smile and take a deep breath.</u>**

These two deeply personal events represent your goal as a budding author, and our goal for you as a result of taking these lessons seriously. So, let's

'Get with it', choose the Cutting Edge - Write and publish your book soon!!! **On that note . . .**

Lesson 2's approach is to move you into the Inner Folds of Writing as we <u>explore deeper with the Essential Steps you need to reach this first time publishing goal</u>.

Let's start with '<u>growing and perfecting your writing</u>'. To bring this into clear understanding we will expand on the **'Power of Seven'** so that you will appreciate its significance and use:

The <u>Power of Seven</u> evolves with your 'belief it exists'. Let's initiate its use by picking the right genre' for you, and deciding the storyline of the book.

➢ **<u>First</u> – And foremost - <u>How do you pick the right genre</u>'? Here are <u>essential guidelines</u>:**

Define your genre' – You have a notion - <u>romance, history, a how-to-do-book, storytelling, mystery, spiritual, inspirational, family stories - real or fiction.</u> Your future readers will favor your fine use of one of these genre'. They search for your next book to buy and enjoy looking under this genre'.

<u>To declare a genre' reflect on your motivation that brought you this far to write a book and examine your own heart</u>. Look all around you and let it emerge. Then evaluate your choice with notes in

your iPhone or an outline in your PC – See what genre' fits.

((Clue – When I began, I looked out in the world and decided for my readers I would bring them inspiration and happy endings – no ugly stuff))

> **Second - Start your 'author's plan' to map out your chosen genre' story**

This plan is to '**list your characters**' and build a '**Table of Contents**' – Know they will both evolve. Take a couple of days, maybe a week, let it unfold.

Why? – While declaring your genre' look around, viewing either 'reality' or 'your mind's eye', begin to see, define and name your characters. See your storyline locations take shape. Make more notes.

As I promised, let me elaborate on this point. By visualizing and visiting with your characters early-on, you will engage with them and begin to sense the '**chapters needed**' to tell their story; and move toward desired highlights and finishes for your readers. Amazingly, as you do this numerous times, you will build the Table of Contents (TOC).

The TOC will surely ebb and flow as the story matures. You are initializing a vital road map.

((**Clue** - I am fortunate to have done a great deal of traveling. I have met many people generating many ideas. *Nine Lives, Nine Loves* came from viewing an Asian family - mom, dad, daughter and son, in a mall food court. Chapter 1 came from visualizing the images of that day and those very folks. *Angels amongst Us* came from a three-hour conversation with a very real Russian Orthodox Priest on Amtrak. Both books offer short stories - personal, inspirational, and spiritual growth oriented.))

> ➢ <u>Third</u> - **Now let's look at what I call the mechanics of writing**

These are significant guidelines for you to know and own early-on to become a great writer: As an example, **why is your quiet work haven needed**? I know from school days many classmates listened to Def Leopard or Starship with ear buds in, doing homework or studying for a test. **<u>For me coming from my experiences of composing, I trust my subconscious to feed me the storyline without other stimulus at that time</u>** – an industry secret!

> ➢ <u>Fourth</u> - **Remember declaring your chapter titles – Why? - Let me explain -**

For me these **<u>titles each embody the Characters, a Theme,</u>** and **<u>Story circumstances in my mind;</u>** and <u>with no outside disturbances, there is **a direct**</u>

connection from my 'mind to my fingertips' providing focused writing with the story rapidly coming out on the screen. This fast release of consciousness streaming from your brain must lead to the first of our seven edits - The Number One Edit is very important because you will sort-out, shape and sharpen your intended storyline.

((Clue - Try this in the quiet of the early morning, say 3 a.m. You may have awoken with a scene, characters and conversation coming forward on your mind. Go to your computer, sit down, see all of this in your mind's eye, imagine it on paper.

Simply type as it comes out and then leave it.

Come back, read it in the light of day.

When you awake freshened, you may be amazed.

You might even say, "Did I write this?"))

Yes, you did. I know, I have done this very surprising thing countless times – nice secret, eh?,

---

For my third book, *Awakening in Newcastle*, this surely happened, shaping the very key element of Part 1. So, try thinking 'quiet'. Think **giving your mind a** break from noise. **Think story** - think going with the flow.

((Parallel Clue – I rarely know the specifics of sentences or words spoken by my characters until I'm within a page or paragraph of the scene. Watch for this unique situation as you get into dialogue. It's not unusual; words will come.))

> Fifth - Next suggestion that can help you is to '<u>start short</u>'

What does this mean? Your <u>writing career can start with short stories, not the all-time next epic novel</u> - **Short stories** <u>quickly evolve and can be grouped as a collection</u> or <u>a novel built from short stories</u>. <u>Grow the story with short sentences</u>, as short as possible and, **more importantly, create them to make the point easy to read**.

<u>Go back, lengthen the chapter or story line to add detail about your characters</u>, begin to explain the situation, <u>the time or place</u> they are in, <u>the tension of 'what if'</u>, <u>the point of completion</u> when he/she **got it**, such as the unfolding love between two. **<u>I enjoy searching in my mind for the likely scene to add touches of reality</u>** to these characters.

Build anticipation / suspense, action / reaction, danger, failure / success, acceptance, pleasure aroused. Maintain the **<u>readers' desire to keep reading</u>**, to come back, to buy again.

> Sixth - Stay on point – Avoid meandering, due to possibly poorly related sentences.

<u>Long sentences can cause the reader's attention to die</u>, skip over well-arranged pages. We can all improve on this – **add commas, periods, dashes.**

In other words, stay focused on the linkage of your book - beginning, middle, and ending – Make each important subset of the story clear. Allow your words to vary - happy, sad, hurtful, giving, loving, caring, rewarding, comforting, even challenging. Even still stay focused, carefully interlace your characters' body movements, feelings, and endearing actions for each of them, crafting very intriguing reading for the reader.

> ➢ <u>**Seventh – 'Listen to see if you sound like a pro' by reading your sentences and words aloud. See if you are prone to wander with disturbing ramblings!**</u>

Right here, as example - read these two proceeding sentences, hear how through the choice of words the first feels powerful (**'See if you sound like a pro'**), and the second scares you away (**'Don't wander with disturbing ramblings'**). Get my point? – Significant growth step – Secret? No more.

<u>Lesson 3</u> Now as I promised, here is 'Added Help' in Defining Stories, Book Structures and Publishing Routes.'

Your choice of genre' for your first (or next) book will also determine what and how you gather information, along with how you write the book. Maybe that seems obvious, so let's explore this.

Please understand my writing tips and stylizing suggestions in these discussions are based on my 'storytelling genre'. I often have a cast of many characters who are my vehicles encompassing spiritual and personal growth in what I call *Inspirational Fiction*. My stories typify real-life events, coupled with my imagination.

You can do the same shaping with your book, whether a 'how-to-do-something', a 'historical tale', or a 'teaching' book, each being a differing genre', each can contain a story as well as teaching details. Decide how to present your 'main character' who, let's say is a cook, or a strong individual type, called to lead a life changing event, or a family member turned volunteer, and in turn becoming a hero.

Even though my genre' is built with fiction, I go to the internet often to check for facts and events to awaken a way to weave my main character into my fiction - my kind of research! If you are doing a true story on 'feelings' go to medical or philosophy web sites for words, or cures, or reactions; get ideas and become enthused.

I love building descriptive paragraphs for setting up the scene, including the time of day, the weather, surrounding points of interest; and creating dialogue with my characters to drive the ups and downs, the ins and outs of the story.

You can do this with your story for your readers perhaps as 'interviews' in place of fictionalized talk. Look around you no matter what genre' and include life and people and circumstances. Make it feel real. Let your reader be engrossed and love what he or she is reading. Photos are welcome; however, they are best black and white due to the high expense of printing in color.

A very key approach to the story weave can be the use of 'flash-backs', as well as 'look aheads' where it is obvious to the reader that the author is imagining what might happen or what has taken place and the affect it has on the storyline.

I particularly enjoy bringing more information, history, substance, emotion into a story by taking the reader back to a different time and age with flash-backs. As author, you must be careful with this technique to make it very clear what is taking place both going back and forward so the reader is not confused or feels incomplete on what just happened in the storyline.

In the next Chapter of this short book I have added a grouping of 'Opening First Pages' from chapters in five of my published books. I am illustrating story composition for you using my chosen genre' for differing *inspirational fiction* books. I suggest as you read try your hand for genre' selection for your dream book and take notes, start composing. See what works for you.

Let's end this book building gathering on a fun tip 'how to break-the-block' as a creative writer.

This tip is to assist and **drive you on when you go 'brain dead' or 'draw a blank'**. Read and keep this idea in mind for a later writing attempt:

<u>When you truly believe, you have 'writers block', don't shut down</u>. Take a deep breath. Get up and walk around knowing you are coming back to your PC to try again. After this break and when ready, sit back down, take another deep breath and start typing, **type 'anything that comes up'** - it doesn't matter what you were working on or what comes up - For example

The big black cat, trying to sleep on the back porch, was now yowling at the thunder and lightning. Suzy shook her husband to get him out of bed to let the cat in. Just as Tim opened the back door lightning struck the steel porch hand rail. The cat was not seen for 7 days. Tim slept well after that. Suzy worried about Blackie all night.

Now, your mind is going again. Something in that paragraph will jog you, like the color **black**, or the image of the **cats frizzed up tail**, or **Tim's smile** as he slammed the door closed, watching Blackie and her fuzzy tail disappear.

Lesson 4 – 'Why it is Good to have a Mentor

Nova Publishing's Mission is to mentor you and expand **your quest to become a published author**.

Why are we, as Nova Publishing.org, reaching out to you folks with our low-cost tutoring for writing and publishing?

I have been a student in one school setting or another all my life. Through this eagerness to learn more, I know and I love 'gaining knowledge that expands our talents', gives depth to you and your stories, and equally important gives back to others. This is going full circle in life, while achieving enjoyment of your own creations.

Nova wants you to know that there are web sites out there on the internet that mimic what we are offering; however, you need to examine your 'return on investment' of your hard-earned dollars as Dad used to teach me. **Building your book with Nova Publishing results in a fully professional book at the lowest cost investment you will find**.

Thereafter, your follow-on promotion activities require good examination as well to assure sales received are in proportion to dollars spent to support your writing and publishing choices. Every dollar you spend for guidance and services must be deducted from your royalties that come back from the sale of each book. Our goal is to maximize your royalty checks.

What is my background and my achievements to assist you as a mentor?

- ➢ I have completed a five-year engineering program; however, I have **always wanted to be a writer and author**. I learned how to use a typewriter in high school in the 1950s.

- ➢ I learned Technical writing at Cal Poly San Luis Obispo in the 1960s,

- ➢ This followed with writing and programming logic code for industrial computers in the 1970s.

- ➢ I received my first Apple Macintosh in the 1980s. Once at the keyboard, I seldom used a pencil again.

- ➢ I wrote my first two fiction books in the 1990s; they were companion techno-spy thriller novels entitled *Pure of Heart* and *Pure of Soul* – got a rejection slip as a young author. It was tough, but I loved the books and learned a lot.

- ➢ Published my first inspirational fiction book, *Nine Lives, Nine Loves* in 2009,

- ➢ My second inspirational fiction book, *Angels amongst Us* in 2010,

- ➢ And my third and fourth inspirational fiction, romance and recovery novels, *Awakening in Newcastle, Vol. 1* and *Vol. 2*, published in 2015, and then my 6th, *Encouraging Words*, in 2016.

With this short synopsis are there any questions? **Nova Publishing wants to assist you with our vast experience.** Please catch me in class or give us a call. We would love to hear from you and clear up anything that may still be vague.

Okay - **What more do you need to understand at this point to become a published author?**

We have been talking about you writing your story, and now with all the above having been said, it is important that you remember the business of authoring is divided into two major segments. This train of thought goes back to my introduction in the front of this book about **Gutenberg's Printing Press**. Gutenberg intuitively knew writers creating wonderful and important books would need a way to bring their books to the masses.

I would like to take an opportunity to recap for you here, and reset your thinking back to the beginning of this book.

What we have been intensely encouraging you about in THE FIRST SEGMENT is all about you, your growth as a writer, being willingly to spend concentrated amounts of time digging into your labor of love. As a budding author, after exhibiting great **persistence** writing your dream book, you reach a lovely point where you must present your completed and proofed manuscript to a publishing entity (Who would have been Gutenberg in 1540 – The first man who printed an amazing, famous book with 'type style letters'.) Up to this point we have coached you on how to produce good, readable content, growing to be a 'wanted writer', not a 'wannabe'. Now we are going to convert your manuscript to a commercialized version for the virtual and/or brick and mortar book store.

In THE SECOND SEGMENT, it is all about publishing your dream book during which you and a book seller will work together creating a polished, professional book. Your efforts truly begin to take shape now. This is where the printer's important contribution comes into play birthing your first bound book for proofing and then on to the marketplace.

Depending on who you reach agreement with, your book can be shown on their sales page. For me, for instance, it was Amazon, who I agreed to sell through due to their worldwide presence.

At this point you can think 'larger' linking up with and showing your product on our Nova Publishing & Book Store website, as well as Amazon, and/or Barnes & Noble, with millions of possible readers to sell your book to and for you to become known. Also realize that there are many millions of books for sale around the world; all of which are your competition. So, in our next Authority Book we will introduce you to **Segment 3 – Publicity and Promotion**, to give your book a life in the marketplace.

What can I look forward to from engaging with Nova Publishing.org? - So far, with you coming along for our first 4 Lessons, we have been discussing as a kick-off the writing aspect of your efforts coupled with your formatting of print books - I have been emphasizing for your benefit how this allows you easy publishing online with us as your book vendor.

As a mentor, I want YOU to grasp 'your required effort to write and produce your book's word processing file'. This is the essential 'other halve of becoming an author. <u>**The Template and its use are easy, and something we are glad to contribute so that this stage does not become a stumbling block to your authorship role.**</u>

<u>**The ultimate step of printing' finally takes place when your book file is ready to send off to the printing firm**</u> – At Nova we are well equipped and look forward to walking beside you to load your book up to our printing firm, await their review and approval for printing; and then 'proofing' the first edition book.

<u>It is here that we will take that BIG step with you of advising the print firm you are completed satisfied with the proof copy and 'approve' release of your book for distribution and sales.</u>

Chapter 5

Describing *Inspirational* Structure and Genre'

It is time for a writing 'Milestone' just for you. And this one is to exercise your mind by me encouraging you to go forward with what Mom always said - *'Practice makes perfect!'*

I am, therefore, presenting in this fun chapter - **Reading Visuals** - examples of my writings for your <u>learning of setting the scene, dialogue, character definition, and action / reaction.</u> Please read on and <u>begin to form concrete ideas for your dream book, stretch your minds and begin establishing choice words, sights, sentences, paragraphs and chapters.</u>

Think ahead with me now as you read and visualize making your own ongoing practice runs of what I call - *Masterful Writing*.

My books have always taken form for me based on their distinctive main characters; but really, people not different from us every-day folks. They are the focus of a host of things going on in life that drive the adventures you and I seek. I love to write as it comes easy for me, from my finger tips to keyboard to life, literally unfolding page by page. Lately I am intrigued with coupling my stories with Biblical covenants to gauge my thoughts with truths thousands of years old, well before Gutenberg's press.

The short description of my books is this: They are fictionalized real life stories about times of difficulty, learning, renewal, transformation, tender-love, many hours of joyful travel and adventure, and happy endings. My intent is to offer you characters who will surely make you smile, cry, cheer, enjoy, feel rewarded; perhaps wishing them as friends, and hopefully leaving you a sense of love. These adventures, settings and storylines vary widely, chapter by chapter.

I sincerely suggest you check out two my latest books, *Awakening in Newcastle, Parts 1&2 and Parts 3&4*, on our Nova Publishing.org website. Each time I dig in and produce a new book the content enthuses me as I explore the writing of deep feelings balanced with joyful, fun happenings. Feel this for yourself.

These two *Awakening* books are lovely woven novels that are easy reading sharing enchanting stories and offering uplifting moments of victory, honor, respect and love. These uplifting emotions often blot out the darkness of overwhelming lifestyles. *Awakening* introduces you to three age-old covenants meant for long term benefit for you and your chosen mate.

Our journey starts by meeting Lisa Sutter through who's eyes we see and feel youthful upset and near defeat of growing up in a big city high society way of privilege, entertainment, charity balls, the best of travel, and Kentucky style horse racing. Yet, even still as Lisa had known the joy of family, her drawback was she relied on family members to fill the blanks of conversation, planning, and ceremony in her teens; never learning the ins and outs of relationships. As time passes outsiders take advantage of her vulnerabilities, making off with hard-earned family fortunes.

Graham Winchester, a strong, spiritual fourth generation California rancher, businessman and philanthropist, is heir to rifle fortunes multiplied with his basic cattle ranching and race horse breeding skills. Living a simple life, he seems content; however, being a widower doesn't answer Graham's need for a fully rewarding life. Change is in the air when Graham and Lisa's paths cross.

Awakening Parts 1&2 present you with stunning word pictures of life, friends, marriage and growth to savor. Our protagonist is a horse whisperer, Omar, immigrant from Saudi Arabia, who teaches Lisa to trust again, working with a beautiful stallion as she had done as a teen.

In the second Book of *Awakening* Parts 3 & 4, we read *many* endearing examples of unconditional love, freedom felt by offering of forgiveness often times unspoken, and the teachings of non-judgmental lifestyles.

The *Awakening* stories carry us along in the delightful days of Lisa and Graham's life on the big Sierra Nevada foothill ranch, now their home together. You will join them on their first travels of adventure and charity around the world.

Living a simple, yet unusual lifestyle, Mr. & Mrs. Winchester experience many charming moments amongst gatherings of new people. As they return to the Winchester after a whirlwind of travel, news comes of Lisa bringing new arrivals to the ranch.

With this I will leave a 'good read' for you to find in the continued story of Parts 3&4 of the *Awakening in Newcastle*. Look for hints and clues for your own writing.

We will continue our mentoring with ideas from real authored stories to illustrate structuring for your book. A significant goal is stabilizing your story's far-reaching context, building continuity, and the importance of correct sentence building.

The following series of stories will illustrate tips on showing off the main characters, as well as blending them in as secondary, supportive folks to your storylines. Relish reading and having fun imaging your own stories to come.

For your enjoyment and learning purposes we are going to look at composition, structure, characters and the real art of Story Telling by actually thinking and becoming book readers for just a few moments. Delight at the following 'Page 1&2' examples from my first five books.

Notice I have arranged these together in a group I call, 'Harmony of Light Series'. This is a very good plan for you as it allows making more smaller books, and package them as a series. This is very helpful with marketing on the internet by searching with the authors' related book series.

Now for your last learning activity, I suggest you make a list for each of the 5 Reading Visuals, and include the following observations with your answers to assist and drive your stories -

1st - Your very first impressions of the structuring and story flow.

2nd – Ease of getting in touch with the main character.

3rd – What surroundings did you imagine she or he in?

4th – Did you have a vision of what main characters may look like?

5th – What situation was developing for each main character?

6th – What did you sense about the author's style, methods, involvement with the character?

7th – Did this reading bring your own stories you are planning to write to mind, or push you on as to how you could construct your book's starting Page 1?

Would you have liked your computer to be right here as, possibly, you picked up on a new train of thought?

Please – Go ahead - read, feel your emotions as you shift from one story to the next, and in turn capture your thoughts on paper; maybe even construct a parallel story on your note pad.

I am a habitual note-taker and a strong believer in the saying 'You never know when' . . . In this case 'come up with a thought you would love to use later'!

Enjoy - - - Let us know how your writing is maturing for you.

My best to each of you

~ *Scott*

- Reading Visuals -

Examples of authoring for your learning

From Korea With Smiles

The gangplank swayed in the warm summer winds sweeping down off the San Gabriel Mountains. A young girl steadied herself on its wooden slats and laughed quietly as her feet danced about. It reminded her of the rope bridges back home crossing the rice paddy watering canals. She straightened her colorful red and black backpack and reached for her mother's hand.

The clear blue sky above the Long Beach Harbor offered a mixture of smells intertwined in the breezes. The slender dark-haired girl recognized some of them, but not all. There was the strong oily fuel stench she had come to know too well. It had lingered everywhere on the ship while they crossed the Pacific making her sick at the very beginning of the trip.

Then there was a new aroma of unknown foods cooking in an open air cafe on the pier in front of them. These inticing odors in turn mixed with the characteristic shipboard fumes of stale steam puffing up from the bowels of the freighter and belching from machines with a lot of whirling wheels and racing rope on top of the decks.

But every so often the little girl's nose twitched with a most unusual lovely, sweet, tempting smell. She welcomed it and tried to hold it in her mind like one of her favorite bakery cookies. She shook her mother's hand and asked her what the sweet smell was.

The short pretty woman, continuing down the gangplank, inhaled deeply for a second or two, smiled and replied, "Oranges, Akikko."

"What are oranges?" the girl asked.

"Fruit that grows on trees. Round shaped fruit that gives us the color orange."

Looking about inquisitively and seeing no trees, her next question was, "Where are these oranges and trees?"

"They grow in large fields in long rows. Hundreds of trees called an orange grove. Perhaps we'll see some on the way to your uncle's house."

That made sense to Akikko, mostly. There it was again. An almost intoxicating smell that made her mind now see hundreds of trees like in a dream. She hoped they would find the trees somewhere soon. If this smell is what this new country was going to be like she was happy to be here.

- o -

Reader - This story segways 30 years into the future for a very different conclusion you might never guess. Makes for fun reading. Keep this in mind.

Angel in the Forest

The hour was very late, a little past midnight.

Evergreen trees, boughs heavy with icy snow, presented a forest very thick to the mind, almost a solid wall. It was, however, in this area that the forest barrier was broken by an old wagon road.

Darkness charged forward to engulf every tree, cascading to hide most every passing cloud, and blurring any other objects to the eye. There was only a quarter moon that occasionally glowed through the clouds. Little of its light could be seen or reach the road through the broken cover.

The dense forest stretched for a thousand miles or more in the higher reaches of eastern Russia.

The stillness parted as a lone figure trudged along the road, wrapped in heavy clothing with a sack over his right shoulder, fur hat with ear muffs pulled down and tied tight to his chin.

The thick layers of snow and ice crackled under foot. Breath held frozen by the air. Step after step the movement continued as if a deeply possessed purpose drove the being on.

If you closed the distance on the figure, you could hear talking, singing, laughing, and praying. A man's voice, rough from the cold and scratchy with fatigue, was resoundingly happy. A lovely sing-song tone broke the silence in the dark forest.

Occasionally he would slow his pace, gaze up and speak. Speaking to someone or some entity? Was this freezing weather causing delusions? Was he even sane?

The man would listen as if an answer might be coming back, at times smiling, and then again, began his trudging.

Two more hours slowly faded behind the traveler's determined stride.

At last, mile after mile, a clearing in the woods opened, rambling down to the road. The man stopped, he seemed to know this was the right place. A low-slung log cabin appeared, nestled back in the dark of the flat field, gently surrounded by a fresh, smooth blanket of snow. As he squinted into the darkness an oil lamp flickered, showing a silhouette in the only window made of tree branches and stretched animal hide.

As he stretched to get a better look, Steffen heard his name being called out faintly; and then again louder.

Rebirthing of the Heart

The morning air is filled with notes of lighthearted flute, each note bouncing in the clearing mist, bringing soft ancient sounds floating up and down with the mountain breezes, restful and pleasing to the ear.

Stacks of large, colorful porcelain pieces formed in shapes of vases and bowls lean against each other in laughing disorder.

Food vendors wrap hot marinated maroca, scrambled egg whites and steaming vegetables in flat bread, hawking their breakfast wares.

Silk wall hangings glow bright red, passionate dark maroon and brilliant yellow with woven gold threads bringing a sense of light and peace to the Saturday festivities. A dark woman tending the booth smooths the precious cloth.

And moving with all these ripples of cloth, food, music and multicolored art are early shoppers searching in the open air marketplace for just the right treasure.

The day is to be an easy shopping day with girlfriends, afternoon lattes and pastry at Joan's Corner Café, and as the sun sets later, a summer evening dinner with their dates, except for one.

The petite blond lifts a silver pitcher at *Loren's Antiques* where the proprietor, a wrinkled old man, has set up his open air table.

Her hands run over the unusual shape, its long handle and finely tapered pouring spout. The woman hesitates with the pitcher in midair, asking herself quietly, 'who will I share this with?'

She senses a couple next to her and blushes wondering if they heard her. They smile and turn away. The woman stares after them as they stroll to the next booth, arm in arm.

Lisa slowly sets the antique down and looks about for her friends. The flute music continues quietly, soothing her emotions and allowing the ever-present question of a man in her life to move back away out of her in-the-moment fears.

Honeymoon over New York City

Morning came with another magnificent sunrise. Light crept in between the curtains as the bride and groom awoke together side by side; now under one roof, each knowing great pleasure to be in the other's arms, both sensing the new reality.

Lisa looked up into Graham's beautiful chestnut eyes. He smiles and speaks, "I have never seen a more beautiful bride than you my dear as you came down the aisle yesterday and approached me on the platform. I shall relive that often."

"And you, my handsome rancher man, in your tuxedo, a magnificent picture. I realize this morning how fortunate the two of us are to be together in the hands of God and His covenants."

"You take the words right out of my mouth dear wife. I thank God for bringing you to me, to this home where we have our eternal futures together as promised by Him. And Pastor John did such an outstanding portrayal of God's ways in the wedding ceremony. We are truly blessed and can thank Him over and over again."

Lisa laid there quietly starring into her husband's eyes.

It isn't often that Graham Winchester lies around in bed in the mornings being slow to rise, but today was special, and heralded many more lazy days to come. Lisa too, was reluctant. However she smiles at the rancher and says she's ready to begin learning the ropes and discussing details about the plan for their first trip. With that little challenge of playfulness, Graham feeling no indication from her to move, suggestively throws the covers back and teases, "Are you ready to see what this day has in store for us, on our first full 24 hours as husband and wife here on the Winchester?"

Lisa grabs at the sheet blurting, "If you insist, please show me dear one," tossing the question back, trying to push him out of bed and laughing. "You have been telling me there is much to discuss, plan, and organize our lives around. Let's get up and meet the day head-on. Show me who moves first."

Reading Visuals 5 – *Encouraging Words*

Garrettsville, Ohio - Sunday Morning

A small spiral bound notebook lay open to a smudgy page near the middle. Other pages up front were all filled.

This open page has twenty names on it, each written down row by row, in beautiful cursive.

Ten names were circled and checked off.

Seven were not touched.

Two names were crossed out with the note, 'Sad for this'.

The last name was footnoted with, 'Maybe, check back'.

Gina had come to Grady's Diner alone about 10:30 in the morning and picked a corner table by the windows. It was still gray and overcast outside. The weather had remained miserable.

Two of her prized notebooks had been removed from a collection in a colorfully decorated cardboard box, now perched on the chair next to her. She had opened her cherished Bible to Romans, Chapter 3, Verse 3.

The young woman reads Verses 3 and 4 aloud, quietly,

"For what if some did not believe? Will their unbelief make the faithfulness of God without effect? Certainly

not! Indeed, let God be true but every man a liar.

Gina knew as long as she kept reading these verses she could trust God and be faithful and true to Him.

She reached for the mug of hot chocolate with her right hand, sipping at it, and continued writing rapidly with her left in the second notebook; the one used for planning events.

Gina's cell phone, laying open on the table, rang with the ring tone of *Amazing Grace*. She picked it up and punched the green talk button. First a smile took shape on her young but tired face and then she let out a shout, "Yes Father!" She circled the eleventh name and checked it off. This time, after the name, she added the initials SFG for Sandy Francis Grandlee.

Sandy's call to the café meeting place was to report another teenager who had just declared she was ready to be baptized next Sunday at church. They chatted for a while and then Gina thanked her best friend and clicked off.

- o -

Do you now wonder about the 'next page', what happens on Pages 2, 3, and 4; perhaps all the way into **the next chapter,** and then through all the pages for each one of these storybooks and their characters? This is my challenge to you – get busy, and write, write, write to enjoy and to bring life, intrigue, anticipation, and hopefully redemption and happiness to your readers.

Chapter 6

Who I Am, Why am I an Author

Let's get acquainted: My Author's Bio - I came into this world having been named Wallace Winton Brown, a member of the tenth New World generation of Browns far down line from my expatriate forbearer onboard 'the second flotilla of sailing ships' following the Mayflower pilgrim group. (This is all true friends, no fiction) That second little grouping of ships brought Thomas Brown, born January 06, 1605 in Lavenham, Suffolk, England, across the Atlantic to settle in Massachusetts in the burg of Sudbury, where Thomas started a long lineage of American made descendants and goods.

It is no surprise that 'a wanderlust traveler' was placed deep in my DNA. So, I have taken travel to the max, while all the time pursuing my first career of bringing big and little inventions to life with automation equipment. And yes, I named myself Scott in college; you may have done the same – finding a name that finally suited you!

I was born in Rockford, Illinois, and raised there through the mid-1940s. I picked up my second US state, unaware I would collect all 50, by visiting Wisconsin as a 5-year-old on a family summer vacation complete with a log cabin, an outhouse, a boat, and leeches in a nearby serene lake. Now mind you at that age I had no idea of what a collection even was, nor did I know my 'young man adventurous love of travel' added to future work would first take me to half the states – from there it became a passion to schedule work for travel.

In 1946 my family migrated west to Santa Barbara to escape the '22 degrees below zero winters, allowing me to enjoy my Tom Sawyer days in lush California. That trip west added six states. By age 6 I had toured through 8 very unique states.

I crowned my collection of all 50 with Alaska in 2008 with my two grown daughters in tow. We stared in wonder at a local mother bear with cubs and admired magnificent Mt. McKinley, known as the tallest mountain in the world, so big it looked ready to climb at 10 miles away. To my nomadic ways I added seven countries and three continents.

After five years at Cal Poly, San Luis Obispo and thirty years of worldwide automation design-build projects with results such as making 'baby carrots' from full grown carrots for snacks and appetizers' right here in Bakersfield, pumping 100,000 barrels an hour of oil from production leases to gasoline processing plants, and purifying copious quantities of ground water for use in creating Prozac; something new in my life was taking place.

In 1992 I began to realize my love of travel, my partiality to Mark Twain's characters, and pure joy of Norman Rockwell' Saturday Evening Post covers was giving birth to a new third career of turning my exploring and uncommon project activities into 'creative fictional writing', as kick-started by my many hours of traveling, working, and experiencing life around the globe.

I delight writing inspiring fictional novels now based on truths that my readers can enjoy and relate to in their lives moving with the ups and downs, easy and tough times.

My first two published tomes, compilations of short stories, entitled *Nine Lives, Nine Loves*, and *Angels amongst Us*, were my third and fourth writer's extreme effort towards publication. They resulted in no **'rejection slip let down'** as I paid dearly to have them printed and placed on the big-daddy website Amazon – it was a trill for sure.

So, quoting the well-worn verse, *'The rest is history'*, please turn to Chapter 7 to read about our writer/author based Nova Publishing.org Press.

((Footnote – my first mentor was my mother. She received a Bachelors of Art Degree in English Lit at a women's college in Rockford, Illinois, and became my education guide for writing during our time together, as short as that was ~ 1940s - 1950s))

Chapter 7

Who is Nova Publishing & Book Store?

In the era of 1990s and early 2000s I garnered fifteen plus years of writing and publishing experience by setting out on a path of seriously learning the ropes of producing printed books. I persistently learned how to build my own books with perfect images; as well as the steps that made them ready for printing, and then culminating this process by finding excellent printing houses.

I compiled all this info and added to it the question of 'who would place my marketing information on the internet'. The answer came – The Amazon Book Web Site was an easy first choice – Amazon's printing house would pass my author info on to their parent owner. It was all there with the release of my first two books.

During this time of three years, three additional novels of mine went up on the internet with no outside help, and five new books for four added authors appeared with Nova Publishing's assistance.

Nova Publishing & Book Store has since come to life exhibiting all these books as a part of our own Nova Sales web site collection; finding that all of this activity of web site and book birthed took place with little trauma through using our own **'Success Planning Six Milestone Traits'**.

And as for the last 12 months, we have added unique 'trademarked novelty sales-tool books', and the formation of Writing, Publishing and Sales classes for challenged folks and the public coming to life with Nova Publishing.org right here in our company's hometown of Bakersfield, California.

We are happy to be here for you and share daily with you. I can tell all of you students who are wanting   to   make decisions about your future, there is no better career path than writing and publishing, and no better place than right in your hometown with thousands of experiences waiting for you within an hour or two.

Truthfully (I know - I write inspirational fiction) - There is no place that I would rather be now than right here with you folks.

((Well maybe - the Panama Canal - haven't been there yet, its scheduled for January, 2018))

Thanks so much for coming to class with us -

Scott Brown

Author Publisher Partner
sbrown828@aol.com

Copyright and Trademark Page

Expert Writing & Publishing -
Teaching Authors, Writers, Business
People with Totally New Insights

An educational book for Business Organizations

Copyright 2017 by W. Scott Brown, V1.0
All rights reserved.

Protected by U.S. Trademark Law
This Book Trademark –
NOVA-BTBCB‾‾‾‾‾

Nova Publishing
Bakersfield, California
www.novapublishing.org

ISBN: 978-0-9981933-4-2
Manufactured in the U.S.A.

Nova Publishing - Services

Nova Publishing & Book Store engages with clients for all phases of book and document development, including provision of project management for:

Individuals / groups / classes / seminars

Writing

Art of Writing, Illustration, Document Building and Editing

Publishing

Document Preparation, submission, printing, proofing, approval, sales and marketing

Contact Information

Scott Brown - owner publisher author
3501 Mall View Rd. Suite 115-356
Bakersfield, California 93306
661-394-0000

www.novapublishing.org
novapublishingorg@gmail.com

- o -

Also by Nova Publishing.org
Unexpectedly Atypical –
Consulting Nonprofits with Outside Insights
Author – James Curran IV
Book 1 of 2 - The Nova Strategy Series

It is important to Clarify for You our Concept of

- No Rejection Slips -

This makes us all smile and writing easier for you.

Fact – Major publishing firms have a way to weed out submissions received via mail from you, a new author, or from your agent (lucky you) who pleads for your piece to be accepted for publishing.

Fact – If you are a bestselling author the firm will welcome you with open arms, cut a huge contract, and assign a staff of 20+/- folks to do your book.

Fact – If you are a mere mortal like most of us, they will assign a reader/critic to declare your work is worthy of the firm to go forward with, or NOT. Then the reader/critic will likely request a rejection letter mailed to you with 'Have a nice day'.

Fact – You wait a long time in either case for word of acceptance or rejection, and your chances of acceptance? – well guess! We don't like this at all!

Nova Publishing accepts you as family, we believed you have a story to tell, you have talent, you care to write well and will present us with a great manuscript your readers will love! That's our anticipation - We ask that your books be fit for the family-room coffee table and as we proceed, that **you edit up to 7 times**! This last part is discussed in this book – it's good for you. You may always join a Critique class for constructive input.

Disclaimer for readers

Please Note: This book is designed to provide general information about becoming a proficient writer. It is based on our many years of experience working within the book publishing market and working with publishing organizations. This book is not intended to offer legal advice or counsel. The information contained in this book does not alter the terms of any book contract or the law of the jurisdiction which is the site of any potential claim or suit.

It is the terms and provisions of each individual's book contract that will provide the scope of the applicable services. Because the areas of law constantly change, those using this book for information should not rely on it, and use it as an addition for your independent research.

www.ingramcontent.com/pod-product-compliance
Lightning Source LLC
Chambersburg PA
CBHW060647210326
41520CB00010B/1770